"Surfing is a deeply wonderful thing –
anytime, anywhere and any way"
-Gerry Lopez

INTRODUCTION

This is a guide of inspiration and encouragement for all surfers who don't currently live close enough to the coast for consistent surfing—and maybe never will. A creative collection of thoughts & adventures to help maintain our common love of surfing, no matter the geography of your four walls. If you were compelled enough to read these opening lines based on the title alone, your passion runs deep, and we encourage you to *Never* give up your desire for chasing waves.

At its best, surfing is a way of immersing oneself in nature to dance across its waves. At its worst, an exclusive club of localism & tribalism "protected" mainly for those fortunate enough (through no effort of their own) to be raised near the shore. And from the ancient polynesians, to the California surf boom of the 1950's, to Kelly Slater's three decade run as the greatest surfer alive, surfing has for obvious reasons been inextricably linked to the coast.

Continued

4

However, ocean waves—particularly the really good ones—are a finite resource far fewer in quantity than the number of us out there hunting them. For even the marginal surf days to exist, a whole slew of conditions must cooperate: wind (little to none or from only the perfect direction), tide (best at different spots & different heights & at all different times of day), swell direction (sometimes down to the degree), swell height (obviously), swell period (the right direction with the wrong period can make an all time day a no time day), and bathymetry (fancy word for the depth and shape of the bottom of the ocean floor). And for the truly unforgettable days, it takes far more cooperation. So, it's no surprise we find competition bristling in the water. Of course, waves in and of themselves belong to the public. But with the unbending laws of supply and demand at work, something had to give.

So, for roughly the last 50 years, surfers and aspiring surfers alike have been looking for new ways to supplement the shortage of & *accessibility* to fun, rideable waves. All while staying as close as possible to what it was we all fell for first in the water.

Off the top of my head, a quick list of surf-inspired replacement activities:

- Skateboarding
- Snowboarding (originally called "snurfing")
- Bodyboarding
- Windsurfing
- Kite Surfing
- Prone Paddling
- Skimboarding
- Wake Surfing
- River Surfing
- Stand Up Paddleboarding (SUP)
- Wave Pools (Also known as Man-Made Surf Parks)

While there are many purposes for all these activities (exercise, adventure, & community among them), for surfers they are mainly used to stay coupled to the sensation of the "first wave feeling" we talk about. The irreplaceable, unique sensation of gliding across a moving body of water with only a board beneath your feet.

Whether we think of it in these terms or not, we are chasing a feeling. And regardless of where you live or find yourself currently, and especially for those far from the coast, the aim of this guide is to provide clear direction for maintaining the pursuit of that joyous experience.

FIRST WAVE FEELING

You know exactly what I'm talking about. We've discussed it ad nauseum from the pre-surf, pre-dawn alarm clock to the post-surf, post-beers midnight video edit. Nothing exists as singular as the way we feel on a wave. For years, Billabong's main ad campaign proclaimed, "Only a surfer knows the feeling," and not a single one of us who have felt it misunderstood.

It gives us butterflies before a session and a sense of longing when on land. And it's probably the main contributor to the "surf bum" perception of the 60s & 70s before surfing found acceptance in mainstream consciousness. "What could possibly compel these men & women to drop everything," they'd say, "for a day at the beach doing 'nothing?'" A question nobody asks anymore.

The best way I've found to describe the practically indescribable feeling is a combination of sailing and flying atop a power moving beneath you beyond your control.

It's what separates surfing from not just all other water sports or board sports, but from ALL other sports period. Nowhere else are you tasked to navigate two moving planes. Outside of surfing, you always get at least one static surface. And it is arguably this anomaly which produces the heightened sense of awareness we experience riding a wave. The heightened sense of awareness, in this day & age, we'll do anything to reproduce.

While we won't get into *all* the activities listed above, we are going to discuss the few I believe most closely resemble riding ocean waves for pleasure & delight and which best help keep us from giving up this important life-long pursuit.

Please allow me to put this plainly: *Do not give up the pursuit!*

PRONE PADDLING

Let's start by looking at the simplest of all land-locked surfing activities: going for a paddle.

Best news: the equipment and time-investment are minimal. If you have a board, a body of water, and an hour to get outside, you can enjoy the glorious freedom offered by a prone paddle.

Prone paddling is exactly what it sounds like: lying prone (on your stomach) on a surfboard or paddle board, and stroking for distance with only your arms and back to propel you. Oftentimes, prone paddlers will alternate between lying completely prone and knee-paddling to use a slightly different group of muscles (your back will thank you!). Slipping the longest board you can get your hands on into a lake and heading off for some arm pulls is both enjoyable in its simplicity and useful in its preparation for future days of surf. For the land-locked surfer with eyes on a coming surf trip, there is no exercise that gets you in better paddling shape than, wait for it, *paddling*.

I have often heard folks sing the praises of what a great workout Stand Up Paddling is, and while it is a perfectly acceptable activity, I've never found it to be a fraction of the workout of prone paddling, nor really all that close to surfing.

EQUIPMENT

When you get out there, you want something *long*.
There are boards designed exclusively for prone
paddling which are typically 12 to 14 feet in length
and incredibly lightweight. The most accomplished &
well-known builder of this style of board is Joe Bark.
Though I must say, it is not lost on me the unique
storage requirements a fragile, 14-foot surfboard
demands, storage many of us do not possess.

Recently, I got the urge to start supplementing my
increasingly irregular surf schedule with a hop in the
water for a lengthy paddle. Fewer are the conditions
required.

I commissioned my friend Jeff Beck (not the legendary guitar player, but how cool would that be?) to build me a custom 11' surf glider/flat-water paddle hybrid. Something ideal for paddling on calmer days & exploring coastlines, while still capable of catching a few waves that roll through.

If you follow our board-building closely, you may recognize Jeff's name as we collaborated with him on several beautiful, balsa-skinned surfboards in the last few years. Jeff specializes in both wood and foam surfboard construction and builds incredibly lightweight boards without sacrificing strength.

With adventure from a prone position in mind, we came up with this magnificent 11' glider in the photo on the next page.

You can be sure this board is coming with me for any long stints away from the coast, as we are all almost always near some new body of water somewhere. And though you might not fully achieve the first wave feeling all the time, you will pleasantly surprise yourself with how much closer to it you'll be when a freshwater wind chop/boat wake catches your complete lack of expectations unaware for a little thrill. Plus, the two-fold benefit of exploring new shorelines, while staying in paddling shape make the prone paddling board an important part of the land-locked surfer's regular routine.

If you only get to make a few short trips each year to ride waves (man-made or naturally occurring), it's best not to spend the first half or more of your trip waking up old muscles and getting back into paddling shape. If you've tried it once, you know what I mean. So, use your time away from ocean waves to paddle wherever you can and as often as you can, and stay ready for the next time they're breaking all around you.

RIVER SURFING

PHOTO COURTESY OF: @BOISESURFCOMPANY

Surfers can't help but look at moving water and imagine what it would be like to ride. And that, my friends, is exactly how River Surfing started in Munich, Germany. Surfers saw a portion of the river where the deep water suddenly hit shallow land and created a standing wave. A standing wave does not travel across the water like those created by wind and storms in the ocean, rather continually rushes over a fixed location to create the two necessary elements for riding a board: moving water and a breaking, inclined wave shape.

A good standing wave will allow the rider to point in an upstream direction, traveling back and forth across the wave that will continue breaking as long as the water continues flowing.

A quick internet search yielded the top river surfing destinations in the USA. Among the most popular land-locked towns with river waves are:

- Jackson, WY
- Pueblo, CO
- Lowell, ID
- Missoula, MT
- Sheridan, CO
- Bend, OR

I've visited towns like Boise, ID and Casper, WY where the local government has put structures in the river in downtown locations for the sole purpose of creating river waves for public enjoyment. This probably goes without saying, but any local government that works to bring surfing to its community is good in my book.

For the land-locked surfer looking to stay in the water, participate in a vibrant community, and keep their surf equipment from collecting dust, river surfing has become quite popular and is worth investigating. I have a feeling we are going to see more and more standing waves in the coming years—both by making small enhancements to existing rivers, and through the engineering of man-made rapid waves, with smaller footprints than ocean-style wave parks.

Yes, mastering a standing wave lacks the nuance that comes along with paddling for, catching, and popping up in the ocean, but think about the marriage of the first two activities we've talked about so far, and you are covering a ton of bases for someone nowhere near a coastline.

Personally, I've yet jumped into a standing river wave, but I've certainly found myself spiraling down the youtube wormhole (as you may have as well) of <u>really fun looking footage online.</u>

I put out a call to the Almond community, in hopes of gathering some more first-hand knowledge on the subject from the true pros. And you guys pulled through in a big way.

One of the folks who reached out was Colby, a former California surfer who now calls Boise home. His insights were succinct and relevant:

"I thought being a lifelong ocean surfer would make river surfing easy, but I couldn't have been more wrong. Riding a stationary wave is so much different than riding a wave in the ocean. It's a completely different animal, but once you get your head wrapped around the mechanics of it, you start to notice some things from ocean surfing do carry over: like pumping across the face of a wave or putting your board on rail to execute a turn (or even the Huntington hop)." -Colby Leslie

PHOTO COURTESY OF: COLBY LESLIE

EQUIPMENT FOR RIVER SURFING

Boards for River Surfing are small and compact. You want maximum control over the board, and you want a board that will fit the tight curves of a standing wave.

Based on everything I've heard, read, and can surmise about it, I'll be bringing the 5'4" R-Series Secret Menu the first time I "paddle out" in a river. The small, full outline of the Menu fits better into the tight curves of a river wave and having a rail that won't ding and shatter upon every bump against the rocks is an added bonus. Once I finally get myself out there, and rest assured I will, I'll let you know all about it!

PRO TIP:
WHEN YOU DO DECIDE TO GIVE RIVER SURFING A TRY,
REMEMBER TO ALWAYS, ALWAYS KEEP THAT NOSE POINTED
UPSTREAM, LEST YOU BE SWIFTLY FLOATING DOWNSTREAM.

WAKE SURFING

If you have never seen Kelly Slater's barreling, man-made wave that peels in dreamlike fashion across the 2,200 foot long pool, then this is your invitation to pause and see what 10 years and several million bucks can build: "Kelly's Wave."

Okay, I know you've seen it. But it never gets old! In reviewing his first-ever experience at Kelly Slater's famous wave pool in Leemore, CA, surf journalist Chas Smith summarized it by saying surfing the wave is essentially surfing a giant, well-tuned boat wake. Unlike an ocean wave, where the power is coming from behind, the power of a boat wake is out ahead of the rider.

Kelly's wave is generated by a plow traveling through the water, kicking up a barreling "wave" in its wake. By carefully designing and sculpting the contours of the bottom of the pool, the engineers of KS Wave Co. are able to create the kind of wave surfers dream about.

PHOTO TAKEN BY THE AUTHOR AT KELLY SLATER'S SURF RANCH IN LEMOORE, CA

Why am I starting our chapter on wake surfing & not the Wave Pools section down below by discussing Kelly's made-made masterpiece? Because every Summer growing up visiting my grandparents in North Idaho, like the wave created in Kelly's pool, we would "surf" behind their boat.

Some of my warmest memories are from those days spent in the country & on the lake. But when you're a dedicated surfer in your teens and early twenties, any amount of time pulled away from the ocean is a real inconvenience. Naturally, I would find every opportunity to emulate surfing behind my grandpa's boat. We would grab old kneeboards, rented SUP's, and most fun of all: the homemade wooden alaia.

ALAIA:

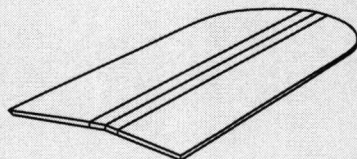

AN ALAIA IS A MODERN ADAPTATION OF
ANCIENT A HAWAIIAN POLYNSIAN SURF CRAFT.
SPECIFICALLY, A THIN, FINLESS, WOODEN SURFBOARD.
DESPITE THEIR LACK OF FLOTATION,
THEY ARE CAPABLE OF SLIDING QUITE EFFORTLESSLY
ALONG THE SURFACE OF A WAVE.

The first Summer it occurred to me to build an alaia for wake surfing was 2008, and I glued together some pine fence boards, cut a rough outline, sanded some basic contours into the bottom, and the result was my 6'6" Wake Surfing Alaia.

It was thrilling and novel. Crude and simple. A little clumsy, yet free. Having no rocker and only some melted candle wax on the deck for traction, we celebrated every ounce of success. That first wooden alaia quickly banished the wakeboard (and its over-tight bindings) from its place inside the boat to its permanent retirement in the attic.

I realized after that glorious Summer that 6'6" was entirely unnecessary, because I didn't need the length to paddle into waves. All that extra wood up front never touched the water, and if it did, we were headed up over the nose. So the next Summer, learning from our experience, we built a new and improved 4'6"!

YOUR AUTHOR, RIDING A HOMEMADE ALAIA, CIRCA 2009.

Building this simple wooden board and towing around
behind my grandpa's boat was a simple, but powerful
reminder of the beauty achieved in the simplicity of
riding a wave.

Years later, I was happy to find not only was I far from
the only person trying to emulate surfing behind a
boat, but others had it far more dialed in. I met a crew
from Austin, Texas, using traditional surfboards to
push limits on a boat wake.

Meet Tegan Gainan, to me, the best of them all.
Mutual friend Evan Adamson—another Texan who
has spent many Summers out here in California—
introduced me to Tegan through his amazing video
work of the Austin wake surfing scene. Go see for
yourself, Tegan and his friends are as proficient at
wake surfing as anyone you'll find.

What makes this Austin crew unique is their choice of equipment.

Rather than doing pop-shuvits & the like on boards resembling skimboards made for fresh water action, they ride what we ride at the beach: longboards, twin fins, and quads. Talk about emulating the surf experience away from the sea!

A couple years ago, I joined Tegan and his friends for a surf behind the boat, and I'm here to humbly report, it is *not* as easy as they make it look. Being accustomed to ocean waves, I was surprised by how fast and critical the pocket of the wave is. They kindly made me feel I was doing great for a first timer, but I have a loooong way to go to catch up to these noseriding experts.

To give you a true insider's perspective, I caught up with Tegan to ask him a few questions about what it takes to get started & to grab some important tips for riding a boat wake.

TEGAN GAINAN RIDING THE 5'4 SECRET MENU

HOW DID YOU GET STARTED RIDING LONGBOARDS ON A BOAT WAKE?

It was definitely a progression. When I was young, we started out shortboarding behind the boat with a long rope. Very few people were "wake surfing" back then, so we copied what we saw wakeboarders doing. As I got a little older, I started surfing more on the Texas Coast. I was really getting into longboarding at the time, because when you are a surfer in Texas, a longboard keeps you in the water a lot more days a year. It didn't take long before my love of riding a longboard on the coast influenced the way I approached riding a boat wake. So, the transition to longboarding behind the boat was a logical one, and once I tried it, I was hooked. I probably haven't shortboarded behind the boat more than 12 times since then. Longboarding and noseriding became the aim.

HOW OFTEN NOW DO YOU MAKE IT TO THE COAST TO SURF OCEAN WAVES?

These days, with a kid at home, I'm lucky to make it to the coast 6 times per year. Timing a swell and keeping an eye on the forecast is a critical part of being a Texas surfer. When the waves are good, the window of opportunity is usually pretty short, so you have to be on it and ready to strike, and that's not as doable in this phase of life.

DOES SURFING A BOAT WAKE SCRATCH THE ITCH FOR YOU DURING LONG STRETCHES WHEN YOU AREN'T MAKING TRIPS TO THE COAST?

Yeah, it's a great short term fix. Immediately afterward, I feel just as good as right after a great surf. But the relief and refreshment doesn't last as long after wakesurfing as it does after an ocean surf. It's a wonderful alternative but also helps me appreciate any opportunity I have to be in the water.

TEGAN GAINAN WITH AN EXTENDED NOSERIDE IN
THE POCKET OF A BOAT WAKE.

ANY EQUIPMENT SUGGESTIONS FOR FOLKS WHO ARE LOOKING FOR A GOOD BOAT-WAKING NOSERIDER?

If you're truly trying to noseride, you definitely need a fuller, wider nose and tail. Especially if noseriding behind the boat is fairly new, you want a big, stable board under your feet. The wake is pretty soft, so more board = more forgiveness.

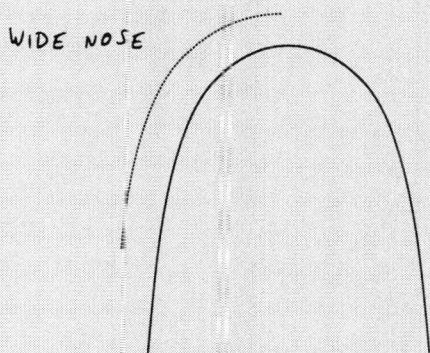

WIDE NOSE

I REMEMBER THERE BEING A UNIQUE EMPHASIS ON THE SPEED OF THE BOAT TO DIAL IN THE WAKE JUST RIGHT. ANYTHING YOU CAN SHARE?

Oh, this is a critical one I see people get wrong. You want the boat going 1/2 MPH faster than you would when shortboarding behind the boat, which may not sound like much, but it's significant.

The goal of the driver is both to make the wave as tall as possible with a pocket as long as possible. You don't want a tall wake with a short pocket. So when judging wave quality, look for length of wave more than height of wave. It also allows you to ride further back from the boat when the wave is longer and that's important for a little extra safety.

But just like surfing, a variety of conditions come into play: boat speed, wind, the amount of weight in the boat, the distribution of weight in the boat, and the hull shape. All have a big impact on the quality of the "wave."

ANY OTHER HOT TIPS OR PARTING WISDOM FOR LAND-LOCKED SURFERS?

Don't leave the coast, haha! Nothing can take the place of ocean waves, but I love Austin. I have a very happy life here. And if you can find that replacement activity you love, it goes a long way toward filling the coastal void & staying ready for the next trip!

THE BEST SURFBOARDS FOR WAKE SURFING

The beauty of wake surfing is you can ride an amazingly broad range of equipment. So far in this guide, we've touched on 4'2" wooden alias all the way up to 9-foot-plus traditional noseriders.

Naturally, my bias will always lean toward keeping wake surfing closest to ocean surfing. The aim of this guide is, after all, maintaining your lifelong desire for chasing waves no matter where you live.

Take, for example, Rob Schoenborn here. He's riding the 6'4 R-Series Pleasant Pheasant and fully committed to the surf approach, even opting to pop-up as if paddling into a wave.

Typically, you start with a rope, like water skiing, until you find the pocket of the wave and harness the wake's energy for forward drive. Then, you drop the rope and maintain your own glide. Once comfortable in the pocket, you can venture out and explore different parts of the wave.

COURTESY OF: ROB SCHOENEORN

As in the ocean, noserides, stalls, and cutbacks are all available to you as ways to maintain & regain the pocket to extend your ride.

Since we finished our first model, I have been a strong believer in the R-Series boards as a perfect fit for wake surfing. For one, if you have ever heard the sound of a fiberglass surfboard bouncing around the deck of a boat, you can appreciate the practical benefit of traveling with foam rails.

And when you consider how we construct our R-Series boards with the same bottom contours, fin boxes, rail shapes, and rocker profiles of their respective custom-shaped, fiberglass Almond Surfboards, you've got the perfect companion to achieving really close proximity to surfing ocean waves while behind a boat in freshwater.

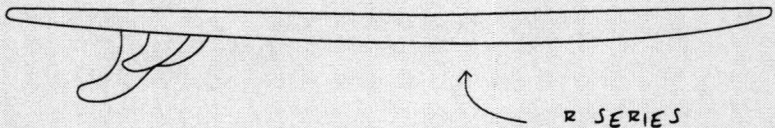

R SERIES

THE FAST & LOOSE 5'4":

The Secret Menu is a direct descendant of my alaia "life lesson" from above by freeing you from the unwanted length so critical to the ocean paddler. A smaller board also puts your back foot right on top of the tail, giving you maximum control. Which makes the 5'4 R-Series Secret Menu my top pick for surfing a boat wake.

Surfers who struggle with riding a board this small in the ocean would have no problem getting up and riding the Secret Menu behind a boat, allowing for the unique, small board experience they might otherwise never experience.

HOT TIP:
YOU DON'T NEED AS MUCH FIN FOR WAKE SURFING AS YOU DO IN THE OCEAN, SO REMOVING THE REAR TWO FINS AND RIDING IT AS A TWIN CREATES A GREAT FEEL ON A WAKE. WE EVEN SPENT A FAIR BIT OF TIME RIDING THE FIVE'FOUR SECRET MENU ENTIRELY FINLESS, WHICH IS THRILLING IN ITS OWN RIGHT. WHEN IT'S YOUR TURN BEHIND THE BOAT, GET EXPERIMENTAL!

HERE, TEGAN GAINAN SOMEHOW MANAGES TO HOLD AN
EXTENDED STRETCH FIVE, WHE GOING FINLESS ON THE
FIVE'FOUR R SERIES SECRET MENU

THE VERSATILE GLIDE OF THE 6'4" PLEZ PHEZ:

Perhaps you want a little more glide under your feet. The 6'4 Pleasant Pheasant honestly never struck me as ideal for wake surfing. But at this point, we have had enough friends argue the compelling case that it is not only a respectable choice, but the *hands-down* way to go. For them I've softened my "less board is always better" stance (a little!), and admit I see the persuasive merit of riding this board behind a boat.

Back to Pleasant Pheasant enthusiast Rob Schoenborn: "Such a blast. It works even better than our actual wakesurfers because of all the volume." Even better than your wakesurfers, you say? That's some undeniably high praise!

When you <u>watch Rob surf the Plez Phez</u> behind a boat, you can almost FEEL how enjoyable it is.

The versatility of the 6'4 also allows you to employ several different surf approaches: you can surf top to bottom, you can cross-step for a stretch-5, and you can use that inside rail to catch up to a speeding section if you fall behind.

OKAY, OKAY, I RELENT. IT'S A GREAT OPTION.

41

NOSERIDERS & LONGBOARDS

If you have the space to bring a longboard on your boat, the 9'2 Surf Thump is a heck of a good time. Although, I will warn you it's nowhere near as easy as it looks to cross step and hang-5 in the pocket of a wake. It takes some building-up of the small, fast-twitch muscles to navigate the often bouncy "wave" kicked up by a boat. Laugh at the falls, practice your cross-step technique, and give it go after go.

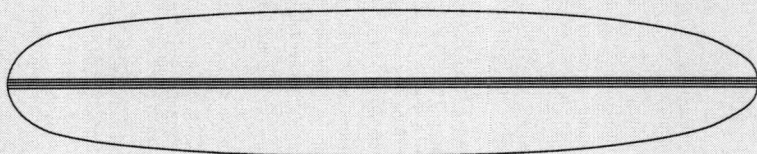

SANO SPECIAL

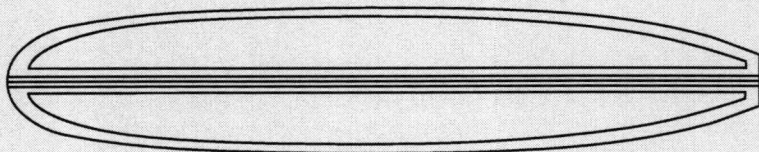

WALKS ON WATER

CLOSING THOUGHTS ON WAKE SURFING:

Another special part about wake surfing, and possibly even more so than the ocean variety, is the intrinsic social experience. Due to needing a boat and someone to drive it, plus your proximity to said boat while gliding behind it, at the very least, you will never be alone. And at the very most, you can keep the banter rolling between rider & onboard peanut gallery through your entire day. Clearly, not everyone wants to be heckled whilst cutting across the lake, but for those who do, the option is always at hand!

Of course, that same proximity to the boat which ups the social quotient, also gives rise to safety concerns which we must not ignore. Always include an experienced boat captain. You really have no choice here, as the quality of wake is directly connected to the skill of the captain, but be completely safe about it. It could mean taking weeks if not an entire summer trading off with your crew increasing everyone's driving skills before any boards are in the water. You'll be glad you did, because the more qualified drivers among you, the more fun for all.

And for utmost safety, wear a life jacket & save the beers for back at the dock.

For the land-locked surfer, wake surfing is a seriously great way to scratch the itch of riding a wave. So do everything you can to make it as true-to-form as possible. Bring a variety of boards, surf finless, noseride in the pocket, and enjoy every leg-burning, nose-pearling minute of it all.

MORGAN LOHMEIER RIDING THE 5'4 R-SERIES SECRET MENU, LAKE AUSTIN.

SURF TRAVEL

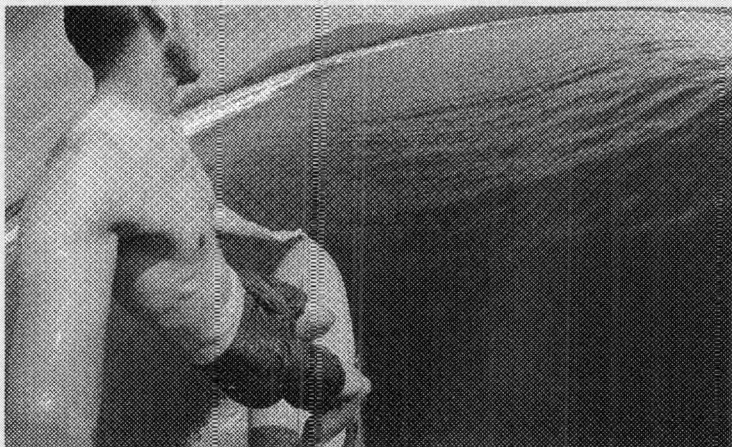

PHOTO: ALEX SWANSON

Surfing and exploration are intrinsically linked. One of my favorite scenes in the iconic surf film, *The Endless Summer*, is when Robert August and Mike Hynson check their un-bagged!! surfboards onto a plane to head off around the world in search of the perfect wave. When they arrive at their first destination, they simply collect their unharmed surfboards from the baggage claim and head off on their journey. With what we endure with airlines these days, it's mind-blowing to witness.

Surfers are forever drawn to the idea of perfect waves breaking on some remote beach and are generally willing to jump through all sorts of hoops & rigor to find them for themselves, including everything we have to go through these days to ensure our boards are protected in the event they're treated in a similar manner to being tossed off a two-story roof.

But regardless of where you live, the attraction of hopping into a car, bus, plane and/or boat and searching for fun waves breaking on an empty beach (no matter how much more unlikely it's become) remains high.

And while you can certainly book a flight to Indonesia, Central America, or Hawaii in search of surf, I'm willing to bet there are waves breaking right now, a little closer to your house. You just need the right plan to go and get them.

Effective surf travel (near or far) simply requires a destination, essential gear, and a good idea of when the conditions there are favorable.

THE DESTINATION:

The importance of choosing the right surf destination cannot be overstated. If you only get to do one surf trip every year—or every few years—you want to do everything in your power to be reasonably assured of getting waves. Fortunately, there are copious resources available to assist in your search. Websites like Surfline and Magic Seaweed offer in-depth analysis on surf spots, as well as live camera streams for the most popular ones.

But before booking any travel plans, you need to know what time of year your destination experiences the most consistent swell with the best weather conditions.

SCREEN GRAB: THE ENDLESS SUMMER, BRUCE BROWN FILMS

Take for example, the nearest beach to our shop: Newport Beach.

While we get waves in various forms from various directions year-round, there are distinctly different seasons for different types of surfing. In the Summer months, the swells generally originate from storms in the South, and we get anywhere from 2 to 5 above average swells to speak of. Summers generally mean punchier surf, left-handers, and waves that are best suited for shortboards, bodyboards, and bodysurfers as they slam directly into our South facing beaches. Finding clean, longboard-friendly surf in Newport in the Summer can be challenging. However, by adjusting your plans even 30 minutes south of here near San Onofre, the exact same swells hit the shore the rolling way your longboards want them to.

In Winter, on the other hand, storms originating from the West & Northwest approach our coastline. They typically bring smaller heights but longer period waves to beaches like Blackies which don't work as well (if at all) on a smaller period, Summer South swell. Critical side note, knowing the curve of a coastline is really helpful for learning which breaks work on which swells.

Rules like this exist anywhere you find surf. If you want to be massively disappointed, plan a surf trip to Rincon or Pipeline in the Summer or Wedge in the Winter. Each of those waves, world-renowned though they be, are radically seasonal.

If your schedule doesn't align with the ideal swell window for your preferred destination, go somewhere else. Arriving at a great surf destination during their offseason in hopes of getting lucky only leads to a sightseeing excursion.

And more, downsize if not outright eliminate your expectations (Pro Tip for life as well!). What I mean is, if you only want to chase empty, perfect lines by local boat transport in distant, crystal blue ocean waters, and you don't have endless resources & unencumbered travel flexibility, the only certainty you've booked are waves of disappointment. If you only have one chance at a trip, pick a spot where swells might not be perfect, but they'll be plentiful.

Frankly, Newport is not a bad option. Though we endure long flat spells from time to time, there is almost always something to ride. Plus, we'd get to be here with you for it!

If you can pony up for an international jaunt, coasts like Mexico, Nicaragua, El Salvador, & Costa Rica are renowned for year-round swells. So, go there. Because, remember, the point is to surf!

Take the time at the start to plot your trip, and you will be rewarded with far more glides down the line & far less wishing you were somewhere else.

THE AUTHOR WITH A 6'4 R-SERIES "PLEZ PHEZ"

THE GEAR:

The ideal travel board needs to check two boxes:
  1. Cover a wide range of potential conditions.
  2. Be relatively pain-free to travel with.

I have paid my dues dragging a 9'6 longboard bag
through airports, onto shuttle buses, and sweating it
out while it's tied to the roof of a rental car—all in the
name of international surf travel. While I wouldn't take
back some very memorable surf sessions in locations
far from home on my 9'6 noserider, I think I've gotten
smarter over the years (and older, I'm afraid).

Now when I travel to surf, I pack a *Pleasant Pheasant.*

Surf plans are often made weeks, months, even years
in advance, so there is no way to know the day-to-day
conditions awaiting our arrival. With flights booked,
dates circled on the calendar, and excitement building
to a fever pitch, you want the confidence of knowing
you're set no matter what kind of waves come your way.

We have worked hard refining the Pleasant Pheasant to thrive in the sweet-spot of both paddle-friendly and lively underfoot. It's enough board to ensure you make the most of those inevitable "two feet & firing" days, and when the waves pick up, the Phez is perfectly equipped to hold a line high and tight in the pocket.

The best surf trips pack tons of waves into a short amount of time, and the 6'4 fiberglass or R-Series Phez will keep you surfing no matter what comes at you from the horizon or the wave pool wall. And like me, it just might become your favorite new travel companion.

WEEKEND SURF CAMPING

PHOTO: JEFFREY ALLEE

Speaking of a drive up (or to) the coast, surf travel does not require an exotic location, foreign country, or even an airplane to be successful.

Perhaps you live 2-3 hours from the nearest surf break, like my friend Greg.

Greg works in environmental sustainability at a well-known outdoor recreation company in the Seattle, WA area.

If you ask Greg, he taught me how to surf when we were young. A point I hotly contest, he's inarguably one of my oldest friends.

Living 2+ hours from his favorite Pacific Northwest surf spot, getting in the water requires a different level of planning, preparation, and commitment than it did when he was growing up in Newport Beach. Instead of a quick surf before work or after school, surfing is now a weekend-long, camping-centric, mini-getaway. I caught up with Greg to ask him for some tips for the weekend surfer.

DESCRIBE WHAT GOING SURFING LOOKS LIKE FOR YOU THESE DAYS.

I grew up about 5 minutes from the beach, but now live about 2.5 hours from the ocean. These days, going surfing requires more planning, but it's still absolutely doable. I typically carve out a full day or even a weekend for my surf trips, and I try to have a plan B in case the conditions aren't good. It always ends up being an adventure which sometimes doesn't even involve surfing, and it's fun to embrace that.
It's a trek to get out there, but when you're sitting on your surfboard looking back at the rainforest, it's easy to remember why the juice is worth the squeeze.

HOW LOOSELY DO YOU HOLD YOUR PLANS, BASED ON WEATHER, SWELL, AND CONDITIONS?

My plans are typically very loose. I usually make a full weekend of it, so if the waves aren't good I can grill and have a bonfire at the campground, or get a beer, a pulled pork sandwich, and play pool at the local dive bar. Other good backup activities are trail running, hiking, biking, etc.

I haven't found a reliable surf forecast in Washington... maybe I'm just not smart enough to interpret the online surf reports. There have been days where the forecast looks horrible and the waves are good and vice versa. So I usually check the forecast but will often still make the trek out to the coast if it looks even halfway decent.

There was one time I drove 2.5 hours to the coast, walked out to the beach to check the surf, and then got back in my car and drove 2.5 hours home because the conditions were awful. I'm not proud of that day.

WHAT IS ONE THING YOU RECOMMEND TO FOLKS WHO ARE MAKING A WEEKEND SURF TRIP TO THE COAST?

Try to eliminate your expectations and treat it as an adventure where surfing is just the icing on the cake. Even if the waves are bad, if you get to spend the evening with your friends around the campfire, I'd call that a good time. Of course we mainly want to surf, but your attitude on what's happening in the moment is as important to enjoying yourself as anything else, epic swells included.

ANY HOT TIPS OR ADVICE FOR A WEEKEND MINI SURF TRIP?

Book campsites ahead of time! Here in the Northwest, you may have heard that we have a dark, gray, rainy winter. You can surf year-round, mind you, but snowboarding is typically a better option in the winter. It can be tough to keep your spirits up in the middle of a rainy winter, but one of the best ways to deal with that is to book your summer campsite out at the beach. I hit rock-bottom this year around mid-January and I dealt with it by booking my campsite for the Fourth of July and a few other summer weekends.

LAST QUESTION. I HAVE TO ASK, WHICH BOARD(S) DO YOU BRING?

I typically bring all 3 of my boards (6'0" Kookumber, 8'0" R-Series Joy, and 9'6" Surf Thump) partly because I don't know what the conditions will be like and partly because I sometimes go with friends who don't have boards of their own. For those who have more boards than I do, I'd recommend bringing the ones that are best suited to the conditions you expect, or the ones that offer the greatest range of versatility based on the conditions.

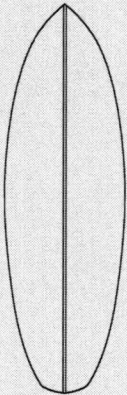  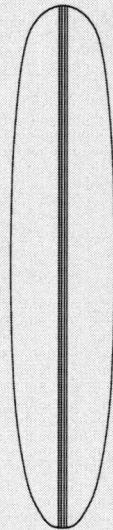

KOOKUMBER   R SERIES: JOY   SURF THUMP

This last question always gets us thinking. As much as we all want the perfect quiver ready for any and every wave anywhere in the world, the truth for travel is most of us have to choose one board. With this in mind, we created the Land-Locked Surfer Bundle which holds a 6'4 Pleasant Pheasant, board bag, fins, and a leash. Everything you need to ensure you're ready for the calling of a distant wave at the drop of a hat!

Thanks for your insight & love of adventure, Greg!

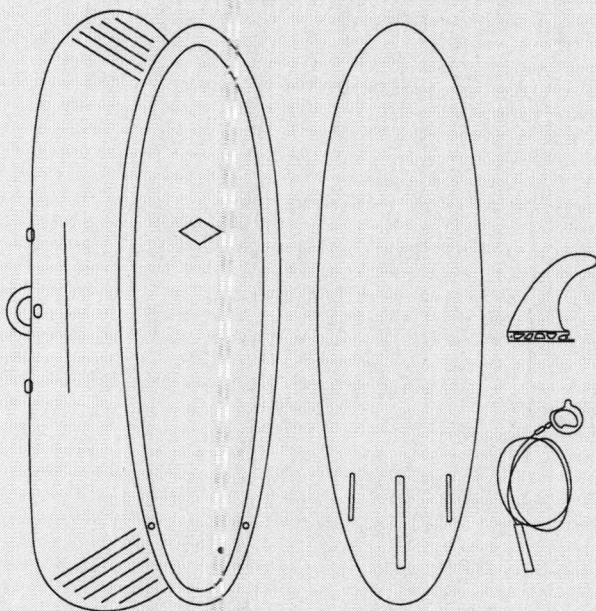

LAND LOCKED SURFER BUNDLE

WAVE POOLS

PHOTO COURTESY OF: ROB HENSON/WACO SURF

Speaking of surf travel, wave pools are a relatively new option for the surfer away from the coast.

As you know, a number of conditions have to align with near perfection for surfing to be possible, not least of all our schedules. There have been so many times I've wanted to just wash off the long of the day with a surf (you know the days), but there was absolutely no surf to be had.

As such, I have long been fascinated with the idea of man-made waves. Certainly not as a replacement for surfing in the ocean, but as a complement to it. I'm guessing you're most likely the same.

In fact, we're all the same. For nearly as many years as surfers have been searching the far reaches of the globe for wave perfection or blankly staring at their dead-flat local break, we've been dreaming of a perfect man-made wave.

Enter the surf park.

THE NOW-RETIRED NLAND SURF PARK, AUSTIN, TX

Surf parks are clearly not the same as finding an empty, undiscovered wave breaking on a beautiful, remote beach. But finding that elusive unicorn is like tripping over a giant nugget of gold while out on a hike—sure it's happened, but not to most of us & not in many years.

If you live far from the beach and spend countless hours dreaming of a few fun, rideable waves to yourself, one of the surest ways to stack the variables in your favor is to visit a man-made surf park. Engineers and hospitality experts have worked tirelessly to create an enjoyable experience, by controlling all the variables required to produce good waves in a pool. And with some added amenities to boot!

If you are going for sheer numbers of waves ridden per hour (or day), a wave pool is nearly impossible to beat.

I spoke about this in greater detail in "Almond's Guide to Your First Year of Surfing." but my surprising wave pool experience took place at the now defunct NLand Surf Park in Austin, TX. I booked an hour on the intermediate-advanced wave in the morning, and at the advice of a friend, another hour on the beginner wave in the afternoon.

The "advanced" wave was pretty fun, probably because of the novelty of riding my first machine-produced wave. I think each surfer got 4 waves in an hour, two lefts and two rights. The "beginner" wave, on the other hand, was a rolling Waikiki-esque party wave of which you caught something more in the range of 24 rides in an hour. For the rolling-nature of the wave, it was not slow, and you would surf the entire length of the pool—often dodging other patrons falling in front of you. By the time you kicked out of the wave at the opposite end, it was already time to spin around and paddle hard to get in position for the next wave returning you back the other way.

It may have been a knee-high party wave, but it's a 150-yard ride, followed immediately by another, and then another, and then another. I wrote in my recap immediately after...

"BY THE END OF THE SESSION, YOU'RE BARELY ABLE TO GET BACK INTO POSITION BEFORE THE NEXT WAVE STARTS UP AGAIN. IT'S ABOUT AS MUCH SILLY, JOYOUS FUN AS YOU'RE LIKELY TO HAVE SURFING. LIKE ACHING LEGS AND BELLY LAUGHS FUN."

PHOTO COURTESY OF: @WRK2SRF

Why am I telling you all of this about a wave that doesn't exist anymore? Because I realized something during that one hour surf session: *Nowhere in the ocean—even on the best day—are you catching anywhere near 24 good waves in an hour.*

Sure, the nuances of a man-made wave differ from an ocean wave, but the number of reps you get greatly, and *I do mean greatly*, shortens your learning curve. You can pack weeks worth of practice into an hour, where you might spend less than 30 seconds actually standing on your board in a one hour session at your home break. I know, that doesn't sound real.

As of this writing, there are dozens of wave pool projects in various stages of development across the globe—with dozens more rumored, or yet-to-be-announced. I read WavePoolMag.com to keep an eye on all the new wave pool projects coming down the pipeline.

Wave pools may seem like a bit of a stretch as a viable option for the land-locked surfer in 2022, however we're rapidly approaching a future where hundreds of millions of dollars are being invested, banking on the fact that these surf parks are going to be a real part of the global surf experience real soon. And with each new pool comes new technology and all kinds of variety. If you are planning on any surf travel to scratch the itch, with the level of consistency, wave dependability, and unmatchable ratio of actual time surfing to time spent in the water, a man-made surf park has to receive your consideration.

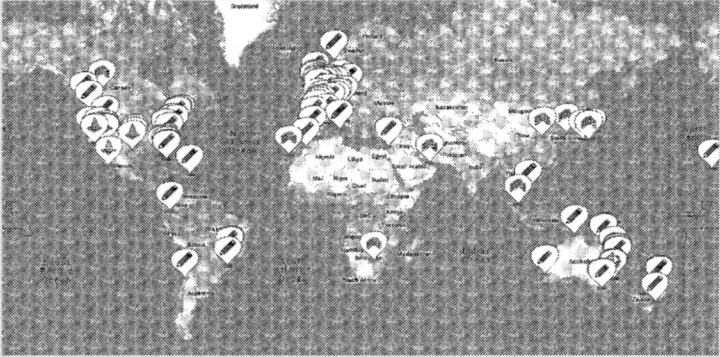

SURF FILMS

Few things capture the whole surfing experience quite like a full-length surf film. When the water feels impossibly distant, a well-made surf film has the unique ability to transport you back to the beach.

Even after close to 25 years, I'm still surprised by how close to suiting up & paddling out a really great surf film feels. And I do mean *surf film*, because there is something irreplaceable about how the medium marries great surfing, great music, a narrative, and an organic, analog moment in time even when compared to the almost daily barrage of contemporary drone or GoPro footage available. Not to take anything away from the amazing perspectives we get from a drone or handheld these days, but the feeling of film is special.

I don't know, call me old-fashioned, but you can retrace the decades of surf culture through the lens of some of surfing's most celebrated film makers. Bruce Brown, Taylor Steele, Chris Malloy, Thomas Campbell, and others have heavily informed much of the way we all interpret surfing.Surf films capture the experience in a deep, soul-touching way that mindlessly scrolling through 35-second clips on instagram can never touch.

When you find yourself in long seasons spent far from the beach, the portal of great surf films will always be at your fingertips to transport you into the lineup & keep the passion alive. Staying mentally engaged with the power of the ocean and the art of riding its waves will ensure that you are never too far away from the next duck-dive, bottom turn, or enthusiastic kick-out at the end of a long one! And if you don't own nor know how to get access to surf films, consider www.thesurfnetwork.com as a great resource. Pretty sure they've got all the ones you want in one place!

"BUT WHAT ABOUT...?"

So, why didn't we cover the other activities?

Body surfing, bodyboarding, and skimboarding, as
fun as they can be, don't fit our criteria for this guide,
because they require access to the beach. And while
they allow the rider to take advantage of conditions
less desirable for surfing, they are unique to the ocean.

Windsurfing and kite surfing, on the other hand, are
activities that I have purposefully avoided in my life.
I have a good friend who is an avid kite surfer, and
respect him though I do, his stories only affirm my
stance as a committed bystander when it comes to
strapping myself into a board & harness to wrangle the
power of wind. Our purpose here was to lend advice
to land-locked surfers looking to emulate the surf
experience, and capturing wind is a different ballgame
than capturing waves of moving water.

Skateboarding and Snowboarding are arguably the most complementary activities to surfing, but have deviated from their origins as a surf-inspired activity and have established their own cultures, industries, and history entirely removed from their one-time surfing roots. Though I will say, the right surf-oriented skateboard can be a great way to practice technique while on land.

One potential "land-locked" activity that came up in my call for content from the community was freshwater surfing on the Great Lakes. I have a tremendous amount of respect for you saltless brothers & sisters, and your dedication to developing semi-pro meteorologist status while waiting on the right combination of wind and weather to generate rideable waves. However, as I tried to figure out where surfing the "third coast" fits into this guide, I came to the conclusion it more closely resembles surfing the Ocean than being truly land-locked and in need of ways to supplement the surf experience. Though, yes, wildly fickle, you still live within relative proximity to the coast, even if it happens to be in Wisconsin or Michigan. Third Coast surfers, hear me now, we support you 100%! We just need to wait for another opportunity to celebrate your commitment to your craft.

SEE YOU OUT THERE:

My sincere hope is that wherever you find yourself,
surfing and dreaming of empty waves will remain a
part of your life for as long as you live.

Be encouraged by the fact that there are more options
available to the land-locked surfer than at any other
point in human history, and there are thousands of
folks investing many millions of dollars to bring the
experience as close to you as possible. So stay ready!
With that said, grab the biggest board you can get
your hands on, find the nearest body of water,
and go paddle.

MORE FREE RESOURCES:

Almond's Guide to Surfboards (Introduction)

Almond's Guide to Fishes & Small Boards

Almond's Guide to Essential Mid-Lengths

Almond's Guide to Noseriders & Longboards

Almond's Guide to Your First Year of Surfing

Almond's Complete Guide to Ordering A Custom Surfboard

The First-Time Surfer's Cheat Sheet

Building Your Perfect Surfboard Quiver

Read More Articles & Surf Tips...

CONTINUE YOUR JOURNEY OF
LAND-LOCKED SURFING HERE:

CREDITS:

Written by: Dave Allee
Edited by: Joel Owen
Designed by: Bread & Milk Studio
Photography: Jeffrey Allee, Evan Adamson,
Rob Schoenborn, Alex Swanson, Rob Henson / Waco Surf.

Special thanks to: Tegan Gainan, Greg Gausewitz, Colby
Leslie, McKane Martin, Scott Atkins, Evan Adamson,
Jeff Beck, and everyone who graciously shared their
stories and experiences.

DISCLAIMER:

The information in this book is meant to help you enjoy many years of activity in the water. Rivers, Lakes, Wave Pools and especially the Ocean can be dangerous and powerful; please proceed with caution and respect any time you enter the water.

The author, Almond Surfboards, LLC, and all contributors to this resource absolve themselves from any legal responsibility for injuries that may occur while participating in the activities described in this book. Enter the water with respect—and at your own risk. Be a student of the art of wave riding, and enjoy the activity for many years to come.